SUMMARY

OF

BEST SELF

BE YOU, ONLY BETTER
BY MIKE BAYER

BY

BookNation Publishing

COPYRIGHT

This publication is protected under the US Copyright Act of 1976 and other applicable international, federal, state, and local laws. All rights are reserved, including resale rights. You are not allowed to reproduce, transmit or sell this book in parts or in full without the written permission of the publisher. Printed in the USA. Copyright © 2019, BookNation Publishing.

DISCLAIMER

This book is a summary. It is meant to be a companion, not a replacement, to the original book. Please note that this summary is not authorized, licensed, approved, or endorsed by the author or publisher of the main book. The author of this summary is wholly responsible for the content of this summary and is not associated with the original author or publisher of the main book in any way. If you are looking to purchase a copy of the main book, please visit Amazon's website and search for "Best Self *by Mike Bayer*".

TABLE OF CONTENTS

CHAPTER 1: DISCOVERING YOUR BEST SELF 12

    KEY TAKEAWAYS 12

- Irrespective of the situation you might be experiencing, you are neither better off nor worse off than people around you. Even when you are way below your desired standard, you are still okay as you are. And this is because you can only be you and not someone else. 12

- The best way to understand if we are living in alignment with our true selves is to take a closer look at our upbringing. How were you brought up? 12

- We are raised within a family structure which has its own fundamental values that are usually hoisted upon us without any necessity to first seek our permission. And sometimes these fundamental values eventually clash with our own personal values and best self. 12

- The womb marks the beginning of our foremost relationship and that is with the woman who gave birth to us, our mother. 12

- Take a look at your journey from childhood to adulthood; at what point, in all of its phases, were you taught how to connect with your best self? Did your parents or friends ever teach you that? Were you ever taught that in school? 13

- We define our personality and identity through our life experiences and the things happening around us. 13

- There are many societal rules that are not applicable to our lives. By spending our energy trying to fit into those societal expectations, we are only wasting the time that we should spend discovering and connecting with our best self. 13

- What we see in the external human world is a direct reflection of what goes on underneath the human mind. Your ability to control your inner thoughts will lead you to desirable behavior and circumstances. 13

- Identify and write down all the best traits, features and authentic feelings about yourself. This will help you to recognize your best self. 13

- Confront all the behaviors and thought patterns that are negatively impacting your life, and that are hindering you from growing and becoming what you were created to be. You need to release and replace them with positive traits. 13

- Gratitude is an indispensable way to connect with your best self. 14

- You can create a gratitude list to include family, job, friends, religion, education, and so on... 14

- Since our anti self works in contradiction to our best self, to reduce its effect and power over us, we need to identify and recognize it. 14

- SUMMARY 14

CHAPTER 2: UNDERSTANDING YOUR ANTI SELF 17

KEY TAKEAWAYS 17

- Your anti self can be one or many. It is a side of you that is affected by bad things such as fears or anxieties. 17

- It is good to create your anti self just as you would create your best self. Doing so will help you to become familiar with your anti self. It will also help you to identify those things that can trigger the emergence of the anti self. This is, in fact, your first step towards being able to control your anti self. 17

• There is no way we can be our best self all the time, hence the need to identify and acknowledge our anti self. Ultimately, the purpose of identifying our anti self it is to help us to reduce its general influence on our day-to-day living. 17

• Do take the time to write down your character flaws. These are the traits that describe your anti self. Writing them down forces you to acknowledge them and come to terms with them... 17

• Writing about your anti self is for your personal consumption and should not be approached with a sense of shame. Be honest to yourself and list all your shortcomings. Denying that you have some undesirable behaviors is akin to burying your head in the sand. It is a way of allowing those negative traits and behaviors to overpower you. 18

• Besides writing about your anti self, you should also move on to fleshing it out and giving it shape. 18

• Remember to actually draw your anti self and give it a name. You can create as many characters as you want from your identified weaknesses. 18

• You are encouraged to check in on yourself regularly to see if a new version of your anti self has evolved, and then put it through the anti-self-drawing exercise again. 18

SUMMARY 18

CHAPTER 3: YOUR UNIQUE JOURNEY: THE BEST SELF TENETS OF CHANGE
.... 22

KEY TAKEAWAYS 22

- An artist is a person that expresses his or herself through his or her own peculiar authenticity. This is why all humans are artist of some kind. 22

- The only way to feel great about yourself is to live out your best self at every aspect of your life. 22

- The five tools for implementing this desirable change are: curiosity, honesty, openness, willingness and focus. 22

- It is the sense of curiosity that encourages learning............... 22

- It will be difficult to connect with your best self without honesty. 22

- Our authenticity, our best self most likely has been buried underneath piles of life's messy stuff? 22

- Rate your readiness for change on a scale of 10, based on each of the Tenets of Change. 22

SUMMARY 23

CHAPTER 4: IDENTIFYING PERSONAL OBSTACLES 26

KEY TAKEAWAYS 26

- Understanding what is hindering you from getting connected to your core self will go a long way to helping you discover how the hindrances can be eliminate so you can forge ahead. 26

- Fear is a major obstacle we confront in the journey of life. In this journey to best self, it is possible for fear to show up, but I want to help you identify its manifestations and how to handle it. 26

- Immediately you are able to master the art of recognizing what triggers fears in you, you can prevent it from dominating and shaping how your life should be. From that point, you are in control of what happens in your life and not fear. 26

- Write down what your fear is, and what it is keeping you from accomplishing, as well as your plan for combating that fear. 26

- The way to overcome fear is to release it and let faith take its place. 26

- Every time you think, feel, say or do things that are not fully you, that is ego. 27

- The best way to help you recognize any of these behaviors is to ask your friends for a proper assessment of you, and to be ready to accept their verdict and constructive comments. Another way is to stage a discussion between your best self character and you. .. 27

- Do not play the blame game. It removes power from you and declares you a victim. It says that you are helpless. Playing the blame game is equal to you refusing to take responsibility for the things happening to you. 27

- To stay connected to your best self, you need to accept responsibility for the things that are happening in your life. 27

- Your feelings are yours and you shouldn't allow other people to influence them. Realize that all outside reactions are noises whose volume you have been given the power to control. 27

- The antidote to egotistic thoughts is self affirmation. Employ this to keep your ego in check. 27

- Write down several truths about you, e.g. *I am beautiful, I am strong etc.* 27

- By staying focused on your goal and not allowing what people say on the social media to get to you, you're turning down noise. 28

- Adopt a good morning routine for example doing yoga in the morning, having good meals in the morning, listening to music, saying affirmations to yourself in the mirror and so on. 28

SUMMARY 28

CHAPTER 5: SPHERES: YOUR SOCIAL LIFE 33

KEY TAKEAWAYS 33

- The term SPHERES is created to help individuals identify areas of weaknesses and strengths in their lives. It stands for S- social life, P- personal life, H- health, E-education, R-relationship, E- employment, S- spiritual life. 33

- Socializing has several health benefits like exercising your brain to make you smarter. 33

- Your social skills inventory include: ability to send or pass a clear message across, good listening skills, ability to receive/give feedback and handling of emotional discussions. 33

- Anyone that has an extreme fear of social situations can explore the opportunity of getting solutions by consulting with professionals such as a life coach, therapists, etc. 33

- Identify areas that need improvement in your social life. What are those things you need to continue doing? What are the things you need to stop doing and what are the things you need to start doing? 33

SUMMARY 34

CHAPTER 6: SPHERES: PERSONAL LIFE 36

KEY TAKEAWAYS 36

- Your personal life covers your internal dialogue, your passions, hobbies and self care. 36

- Before you can show up as your best self in your role as a parent, or spouse or sibling or friend or employee or role model, you must first show up for yourself, that is, take care of yourself first, consider yourself. 36

- You can change your brain's structure and function by changing your internal dialogue, that is, the messages you send to your brain. 36

- The more compassionate you are to yourself the more you will be able to care for others. 36

- Mindful breath exercises should be done routinely because it helps to calm the brain. This exercise can be done in the morning or afternoon or at night. You can also do the exercises all day, a few minutes at a time. 36

- You cannot talk of passion and still be disconnected from the world and people around you. You cannot live a solitary lonely life either and be passionate. No. 37

- Living out your best self implies being passionate 37

- Pain is an inevitable life experience which we often surrender to. 37

SUMMARY 37

CHAPTER 7: YOUR HEALTH 40

KEY TAKEAWAYS 40

- Other SPHERES of life will be useless if your health is affected that is why your health plays a primary role in your best self. 40

- Your mind is the power house where you first create a healthy or an unhealthy body. 40

- Irrespective of your health history, you can take charge of your health at any time and turn it into your priority. 40

- Our body is like a house whose structures and systems can collapse if neglected. 40

- There is a great connection between your brain, your intestinal tract and your emotions. 40

- The gut microbiome, which is the bacteria found in the gastrointestinal tract, has been found to play an indispensable role in our health. 40

- Food and other supplements going through the gut indirectly feed the mind, which indirectly affects your entire mood and behavior. 40

- Your diet can be tweaked to help your thinking and mood and to give you the energy you need to become your desired best self. 41

- There is a need for you to reexamine your beliefs around diet and nutrition. 41

- The type of meals you eat determine whether you are fueling your anti self or your best self. 41

- Fermented food like kombucha is recommended as the type of food to incorporate into your daily diet in order to become your best self. Other recommendations are probiotic supplements, sauerkraut, kefir, unsweetened yoghurt and fiber. Also try to eat an apple daily. 41

- Interval fasting is also recommended as it induces autophagy. Autophagy is a situation where the body consumes its own tissue through a sort of recycling by using the waste produced by the body to create new materials needed for regeneration of the cells. 41

- Exercise is of numerous critical benefits to the human body, brain and spirit. Exercise is a key element in becoming your best self. 41

SUMMARY 41

- CHAPTER 8: YOUR EDUCATION/ LEARNING 44
  - KEY TAKEAWAYS 44
  - SUMMARY 45
- CHAPTER 9: YOUR RELATIONSHIPS 48
  - KEY TAKEAWAYS 48
  - SUMMARY 49
- CHAPTER 10: YOUR EMPLOYMENT 52
  - KEY TAKEAWAYS 52
  - SUMMARY 53
- CHAPTER11: YOUR SPIRITUAL LIFE 54
  - KEY TAKEAWAYS 54
  - SUMMARY 54
- CHAPTER 12: ASSEMBLING YOUR BEST TEAM 56
  - KEY TAKEAWAYS 56
  - SUMMARY 57
- CHAPTER 13: SEVEN STEPS TO ACQUIRING YOUR BEST SELF GOALS 58
  - KEY TAKEAWAYS 58
  - SUMMARY 58
- CONCLUSION 60
  - KEY TAKEAWAYS 60
  - SUMMARY 60

NOTES..61

CHAPTER 1: DISCOVERING YOUR BEST SELF

KEY TAKEAWAYS

- Irrespective of the situation you might be experiencing, you are neither better off nor worse off than people around you. Even when you are way below your desired standard, you are still okay as you are. And this is because you can only be you and not someone else.

- The best way to understand if we are living in alignment with our true selves is to take a closer look at our upbringing. How were you brought up?

- We are raised within a family structure which has its own fundamental values that are usually hoisted upon us without any necessity to first seek our permission. And sometimes these fundamental values eventually clash with our own personal values and best self.

- The womb marks the beginning of our foremost relationship and that is with the woman who gave birth to us, our mother.

- Take a look at your journey from childhood to adulthood; at what point, in all of its phases, were you taught how to connect with your best self? Did your parents or friends ever teach you that? Were you ever taught that in school?

- We define our personality and identity through our life experiences and the things happening around us.

- There are many societal rules that are not applicable to our lives. By spending our energy trying to fit into those societal expectations, we are only wasting the time that we should spend discovering and connecting with our best self.

- What we see in the external human world is a direct reflection of what goes on underneath the human mind. Your ability to control your inner thoughts will lead you to desirable behavior and circumstances.

- Identify and write down all the best traits, features and authentic feelings about yourself. This will help you to recognize your best self.

- Confront all the behaviors and thought patterns that are negatively impacting your life, and that are hindering you from growing and becoming what you were created to be. You need to release and replace them with positive traits.

- Gratitude is an indispensable way to connect with your best self.

- You can create a gratitude list to include family, job, friends, religion, education, and so on.

- Since our anti self works in contradiction to our best self, to reduce its effect and power over us, we need to identify and recognize it.

SUMMARY

Everyone is created in a special way. There can never be another you. If you have heard the saying that you are special before, I want you to let it have a new influence upon you. The totality of your thoughts, feelings, experiences, spirit and genetics are all peculiar to just you alone. This is why no one can exactly understand what it feels to be in your situation. No one has ever been you neither will anyone ever be you. Such can never happen.

At the point of your birth, there were some unique traits and innate characteristics that differentiated you from others. In a similar vein, you are a carrier of some peculiar genes inherited from your parents and although infinitesimal, your DNA is another aspect of your inherent traits.

We all have stories that begin at birth. All of us were influenced by people around us as we powerlessly allowed them to write whatever they wanted on our blank slates. There is the need to revisit our original stories to know if as adults, we are living our lives in alignment with who we were supposed to be or perhaps to discover what negative impact our past might be having on us, in the present.

Since family values are dynamic and vary, there are some fundamental values from the family that do not align with our personal values, thereby affecting and shaping who we are, our personality.

Our mother is the first relationship we have while we are in her womb. After birth, we form relationships with our immediate family members who also influence our lives.

After that, we grow to puberty with all its confusing hormonal changes and rush of emotions. We gradually move on to adulthood and then begin to live independently and to assume some degree of financial responsibility. Religion is another significant aspect of our upbringing. We embrace the religion of our immediate family which we later either continue with, or discard for another.

The skills we need to connect to our best self are not taught in schools, neither do our parents or friends teach them to us. This creates a vacuum. And when we grow up, this vacuum makes us feel somewhat off and inauthentic in one or more areas of our lives.

One of my clients, a musician and a good entertainer was going through a difficult situation after his band broke up. He was struggling as a solo artist, and began to give in to negative thoughts. When he sent for me, I asked him who his hero was. He named his hero "Ralph" and visualized him as a squirrel. He named his antihero, "Minus". Though Ralph was a squirrel, it was his mental picture of his best self which he could build up in his mind to contend against Minus. He decided to consult with Ralph and shut out Minus. Within a short time, he wrote a hit song that got him several awards. Ralph gave him the confidence he needed to sideline Minus and his limiting thoughts.

You can also create your best self, which can be of any gender, or be an animal, or a book/movie character or a mysterious being/voice from within. Draw your best self using a pencil, crayon, etc. Let your best self character you create become your coach and your ideal. With this, your best self character will always be by your side for life. This is a cheaper replacement for a real-life life coach.

Gratitude is a powerful tool that can help you connect with your real self. You can create a gratitude list for yourself daily covering various areas of your life such as job, home, children, health, religion, and so on. Don't forget that the presence of best self is an indication that there is an anti self. The best way to reduce the power of the anti self over us is to recognize it and to deny it any control over any aspect of our lives.

CHAPTER 2: UNDERSTANDING YOUR ANTI SELF

KEY TAKEAWAYS

- Your anti self can be one or many. It is a side of you that is affected by bad things such as fears or anxieties.

- It is good to create your anti self just as you would create your best self. Doing so will help you to become familiar with your anti self. It will also help you to identify those things that can trigger the emergence of the anti self. This is, in fact, your first step towards being able to control your anti self.

- There is no way we can be our best self all the time, hence the need to identify and acknowledge our anti self. Ultimately, the purpose of identifying our anti self it is to help us to reduce its general influence on our day-to-day living.

- Do take the time to write down your character flaws. These are the traits that describe your anti self. Writing them down forces you to acknowledge them and come to terms with them.

- Writing about your anti self is for your personal consumption and should not be approached with a sense of shame. Be honest to yourself and list all your shortcomings. Denying that you have some undesirable behaviors is akin to burying your head in the sand. It is a way of allowing those negative traits and behaviors to overpower you.

- Besides writing about your anti self, you should also move on to fleshing it out and giving it shape.

- Remember to actually draw your anti self and give it a name. You can create as many characters as you want from your identified weaknesses.

- You are encouraged to check in on yourself regularly to see if a new version of your anti self has evolved, and then put it through the anti-self-drawing exercise again.

SUMMARY

I have a friend named Suzanne who I have known for a long time. On day she was caught up in a bad traffic jam while driving home from work. Such was the situation she was in when I called her, although all that was unknown to me. She responded well with no hint that she was under a stressful situation. I asked if we could have dinner on the following Thursday. She responded affirmatively. But as soon as we ended the call, I heard her spew a slew of invectives against another driver that had nearly bumped into her in the traffic jam. Apparently the stressful situation got to her; she lost her temper and started spewing a whole lotta bad language.

Eventually when we met for dinner, I asked her why she had acted the way she did the day I called her. She was surprised because she did not know how I got the wind of what happened. Anyway, I told her that she hadn't switched off her phone after our call ended and so I heard the whole brouhaha. She was so embarrassed.

Anyway, I decided I should have her carry out the anti-self-drawing exercise. She protested at first, but later agreed and drew her anti self who she named "Road-Rage Regina".

Apart from stress behind the wheel, Suzanne agreed that there were also other things that bring out her anti self. She identified one such thing as whenever she begins to feel fed up with a situation. Another anti self she identified is the feeling of shutting down whenever she is in a new environment. Another is when she feels inexperienced and self consciousness. Having identified these anti self (selves), she was able to acknowledge them and determine ways to keep them under control.

Anti self is not fluff. It is real. I have clients who have also confessed to having alter egos. To be more precise as humans who are prone to changes and influences all the time. And as such we cannot be our best self all the time. So the idea behind identifying our anti self is to help us reduce the duration of time we normally spend with it.

Even I personally have a certain level of insecurity arising from some fears I have about how people may think of me. This affects my confidence. But I have been able to handle this better with help from my best self, Merlin.

As a guide to writing your own anti self traits, you should consider the following:

- Do I harbor an unforgiving attitude towards others and myself?
- Am I quick to pick offense or to get angry?
- Do I intentionally make choices that are unhealthy?
- Am I impatient most times?
- Am I a know-it-all person?
- Do I often give up before a goal is accomplished?
- Do I have the belief of not being good enough?
- Do I permit people to just walk all over me?
- Do I act selfishly?

Have you recently acted in such a way that afterwards you felt like you **didn't act well or that you should have handled things better?** That's your anti self at work. Anti self manifests in various ways. It can come as a bad feeling that follows an unpleasant experience (like self condemnation). It can also manifest in the form of story creation (e.g. creating a false narrative). This is a way of interpreting people's actions from your own perspective and different from their intentions. To create your list of your anti self, include anything and everything that you do that you consider bad.

Having identified your anti self, when next it tries emerging from within you, summon your best self to help to handle it (battle of the selves). While this may be difficult to implement at the initial stage, with time, however, sit will become automatic. Your best self will unconsciously be in charge of any situation instead of your anti self.

CHAPTER 3: YOUR UNIQUE JOURNEY: THE BEST SELF TENETS OF CHANGE

KEY TAKEAWAYS

- An artist is a person that expresses his or herself through his or her own peculiar authenticity. This is why all humans are artist of some kind.

- The only way to feel great about yourself is to live out your best self at every aspect of your life.

- The five tools for implementing this desirable change are: curiosity, honesty, openness, willingness and focus.

- It is the sense of curiosity that encourages learning.

- It will be difficult to connect with your best self without honesty.

- Our authenticity, our best self most likely has been buried underneath piles of life's messy stuff?

- Rate your readiness for change on a scale of 10, based on each of the Tenets of Change.

SUMMARY

When I ask people about their art, they become confused about the right response to give. But by art I mean how they express who they are at their core, daily, in terms of their chosen career, interaction with their family members, hobbies, etc.

One of the Tenets or tools for change is curiosity. This applies to just yourself, that is, being aware of your behavior, thought patterns and other interaction with the world around you. The curiosity meant here is not the self destructive negative thought patterns that make an individual beat him or herself down. Curiosity as used here refers to the trait that helps you to see your real self as you are at the moment, in order to know where you are headed to.

Honesty is another of the Tenets or tools for change. Honesty makes us as sincere as we can with our behaviors. It also enables us to accurately classify our behaviors as either part of our best self or part of our anti self. There is a need for you to operate from a position of truth and not from shame or avoidance of our best self. Honesty gets you there.

Openness is another of the Tenets or tools for change. Openness here implies having a teachable mind. You ought to have the mind to learn new things and acquire new knowledge. It will help you to make better decisions towards becoming your best self.

Willingness is another of the Tenets or tools for change. Willingness means the determination to go to any length to achieve your goal and become a better you.

Focus is another of the Tenets or tools for change. Focus means staying on course. Different people have different ways of getting focused. For me, staying focused usually means being in the right atmosphere with less distraction and a chair. You should identify what focus means to you and keep your dream going.

Things that can charge your authenticity battery

A battery of authenticity is charged when an individual goes through moments of complete rejuvenation and feelings of being fully alive and charged. To know these moments, consider the following:

- You must think of such moments and write down things that make you feel fully charged.
- If it's an activity, when last was it?
- What is the relationship between your best self and the identified activity?
- Identify areas of your life that suitably matches your best self.
- Identify areas of your life that do not match with your best self.

Change stages

- Pre contemplation
- Contemplation
- Preparation

- Action
- Maintenance

CHAPTER 4: IDENTIFYING PERSONAL OBSTACLES

KEY TAKEAWAYS

- Understanding what is hindering you from getting connected to your core self will go a long way to helping you discover how the hindrances can be eliminate so you can forge ahead.

- Fear is a major obstacle we confront in the journey of life. In this journey to best self, it is possible for fear to show up, but I want to help you identify its manifestations and how to handle it.

- Immediately you are able to master the art of recognizing what triggers fears in you, you can prevent it from dominating and shaping how your life should be. From that point, you are in control of what happens in your life and not fear.

- Write down what your fear is, and what it is keeping you from accomplishing, as well as your plan for combating that fear.

- The way to overcome fear is to release it and let faith take its place.

- Every time you think, feel, say or do things that are not fully you, that is ego.

- The best way to help you recognize any of these behaviors is to ask your friends for a proper assessment of you, and to be ready to accept their verdict and constructive comments. Another way is to stage a discussion between your best self character and you.

- Do not play the blame game. It removes power from you and declares you a victim. It says that you are helpless. Playing the blame game is equal to you refusing to take responsibility for the things happening to you.

- To stay connected to your best self, you need to accept responsibility for the things that are happening in your life.

- Your feelings are yours and you shouldn't allow other people to influence them. Realize that all outside reactions are noises whose volume you have been given the power to control.

- The antidote to egotistic thoughts is self affirmation. Employ this to keep your ego in check.

- Write down several truths about you, e.g. *I am beautiful, I am strong etc.*

- By staying focused on your goal and not allowing what people say on the social media to get to you, you're turning down noise.

- Adopt a good morning routine for example doing yoga in the morning, having good meals in the morning, listening to music, saying affirmations to yourself in the mirror and so on.

SUMMARY

On this journey of best self discovery, there is the tendency to meet with some challenges that will want to hinder your success. Your foresight of such roadblocks can help you plan out a detour.

The Inventory of Fear Quiz

Fear is the number one thing that gets in our way of progress, telling us all forms of lies that do not exist. Yet, we often fall prey to it and succumb to it. It is possible to let fear stand in your way of best self journey but I don't want it to happen. That is why we are going to identify and tackle it.

Part 1: what is it you're afraid of?

Immediately you are able to master the art of recognizing what triggers fears in you, you can prevent fear from dominating and shaping how your life should be. From that point, you are in control of what happens in your life and not fear. Respond fast to each of these fear quizzes by writing down all that comes to your immediately. Just write and don't hesitate.

What are the fears that have held you back from implementing changes in any aspect of your life?

Part 2: Pattern of Fear

Can you notice a pattern from your written list? Is it possible to group your fears into categories? For instance, your fear may have root in the fact that you're not loved or valuable enough.

Write down your overarching reason for being afraid of change

Part 3: Put Your fear to the test

You are to write down your fears; rational and legitimate. That fear that is hindering you from doing what you have planned doing. Create a plan that will counter it from manifesting in real life. For instance, if you want to establish your business and quit your job, the fear of failing and not being able to successfully manage it could come up. This is rational fear. To combat it, save up enough money to take you for several months before resigning from your present job.

Exercise

My fear is ---------------- *rejection*

It keeps me from_ --------------------- *meeting people, adventuring, etc*

*My plan for combating my fear from manifesting in real life_* ----------------*find happiness in meeting people, to be optimistic about life when rejection comes that it is opening a better door.*

Identify as many fears as possible and apply this test on all of them. With a combating plan for each of them, you're already in control.

Part 4: Faith overpowers fear

You can practice visualization exercise to strengthen and help in having the freedom you need from fear.

- With eyes closed, imagine your fear and the effects on you
- Put them in a big cardboard box in your mind
- Reduce the size of the box into your palm size
- Imagine standing on a height
- Throw the box and let it roll out
- Imagine a shower after turning around
- Turn on the water and feel it's cool sensation all over you
- Open your eyes to a renewed refreshed life of faith

Ego versus best self: personal choice

Ego here implies that fear that has grown its roots in us as if it has been inscribed in our DNA. Ego manifests in different ways such as lashing at others, being involved in a heated argument, thinking you're better at doing things just to avoid embarrassment;

anything done that is not your real self. In this journey of best self discovery, ego might pop up as an obstacle, but this is how to identify it and conquer it.

Step 1: Recognizing ego

There are times we act according to our ego instead of our best self. Ego can be obvious and big and also manifest in subtle ways:

Big/obvious ego

- Being defensive
- The fight to win an argument
- Pride/boasting
- Revenge
- Being possessive
- Talking poorly or crafting bad narratives about others
- Being dishonest
- Bullying
- Having a victim mentality

Less obvious/subtle manifestation of ego

- Seeking people's approval
- Fear of loneliness
- Bullying others as a result of different beliefs
- Criticism offends their pride and instead of accepting it, their pride is hurt and they lash out
- Clinging to the past and relegating others because of their past
- Insecurity and feeling of inadequacy

- Frequently apology in order to be accepted by others
- Looking up to others to define their worth and significance

Refusal to play the blame game

This is the victim mentality, which I often view as being dangerous mentality. To play this role, you (the victim) point fingers at others or things going wrong with you. Whatever happens to us, we have the choice to either accept it and see how it can be prevented from happening in the future or blame others for it.

Step 2: Turning off the noise of your ego

These come in form of feelings of inadequacy, and they are related to fears.

Check out your daily routines as they may impact your life negatively or positively. Choose a mantra and recite it every morning, before presentations and other major activities. You can have several mantras.

CHAPTER 5: SPHERES: YOUR SOCIAL LIFE

KEY TAKEAWAYS

- The term SPHERES is created to help individuals identify areas of weaknesses and strengths in their lives. It stands for S- social life, P- personal life, H- health, E-education, R-relationship, E-employment, S- spiritual life.

- Socializing has several health benefits like exercising your brain to make you smarter.

- Your social skills inventory include: ability to send or pass a clear message across, good listening skills, ability to receive/give feedback and handling of emotional discussions.

- Anyone that has an extreme fear of social situations can explore the opportunity of getting solutions by consulting with professionals such as a life coach, therapists, etc.

- Identify areas that need improvement in your social life. What are those things you need to continue doing? What are the things you need to stop doing and what are the things you need to start doing?

SUMMARY

This chapter deals with the first S in SPHERES which is your social life. The question is: are you always your best self when interacting with others in a social environment?

Social anxiety is not a product of our best self and it can be overcome. People that have difficulty with social communication are those that have some fears/anxieties built up in them over time. To get out of this challenge, you need to set specific goals toward effective change.

A good listener is someone acting from his or her best self, instead of acting from ego.

The following are effective socializing skills:

- Being prepared to share something in a group.
- Being focused and present of mind and not being absent minded.
- Asking questions about other people's families, hobbies, jobs, etc and practically show that you care from your heart and that you are not just putting on an act.
- Being a good listener without interrupting
- Maintaining a bold/confident disposition and posture throughout your conversation.
- Watching your tone in each setting because your tone reflects your words.

- Chatting instead of preaching and knowing when to express your opinions/feelings about a topic and when to stay silent.
- Maintaining eye contact with your peers or group during interactions.
- Giving compliments and positive feedbacks.
- Recognizing guests or strangers

CHAPTER 6: SPHERES: PERSONAL LIFE

KEY TAKEAWAYS

- Your personal life covers your internal dialogue, your passions, hobbies and self care.

- Before you can show up as your best self in your role as a parent, or spouse or sibling or friend or employee or role model, you must first show up for yourself, that is, take care of yourself first, consider yourself.

- You can change your brain's structure and function by changing your internal dialogue, that is, the messages you send to your brain.

- The more compassionate you are to yourself the more you will be able to care for others.

- Mindful breath exercises should be done routinely because it helps to calm the brain. This exercise can be done in the morning or afternoon or at night. You can also do the exercises all day, a few minutes at a time.

- You cannot talk of passion and still be disconnected from the world and people around you. You cannot live a solitary lonely life either and be passionate. No.

- Living out your best self implies being passionate

- Pain is an inevitable life experience which we often surrender to.

SUMMARY

This chapter focuses on your personal life, the important relationship with yourself. This entails your positive self image and the care you give to your own self.

Internal dialogue

This is the summation of the messages you tell yourself. Since you have the power to control your brain through the messages sent to it, you should henceforth, begin to tell your brain the type of person you are as well as the type of life you desire. All these things will manifest in real life.

Identify what you say to yourself on any normal day in terms of what you do, your intelligence, competence, skills and abilities, appearance and self worth.

Also, watch what you say when under pressure. Also identify the common themes within your internal dialogue. Watch out for the tone of your internal dialogue; pessimistic, rational, positive etc. Who is in control of your life? You, others or circumstances of life? Do you live your life for chance to catch up with it?

Self care

Self care entails showing compassion to yourself. In life, a lot of folks find it easy to care for others at the detriment of their own welfare. You cannot give what you don't have. It is when your tank is full and overflowing that you can easily give others. The first step to self care is proper stress management.

How to build personal stress management kits

- Do breathing exercises. Take about 4 deep breaths in and out
- Engage in physical exercise
- Celebrate your life. Don't wait for an anniversary or birthday before you think of celebration. It should be done from time to time. Give yourself a little treat for each little accomplishment.
- Get enough sleep
- Get away from tech gadgets
- Get connected with what makes you feel relaxed.

Passion

This is the third aspect of your personal life. It is identifying things that bring out the life in you and make you have the highest sense of fulfillment. It could be a hobby, a game or any such thing.

For those in pains

Emotional pain is divided into rejection and loss. Pain is part of life's challenges, so we must accept it in good faith. Surrendering to pain does not mean you're losing. There is no winning or losing in pain. Just ensure that you allow comfort into your life irrespective of whatever pain you may be going through.

CHAPTER 7: YOUR HEALTH

KEY TAKEAWAYS

- Other SPHERES of life will be useless if your health is affected that is why your health plays a primary role in your best self.

- Your mind is the power house where you first create a healthy or an unhealthy body.

- Irrespective of your health history, you can take charge of your health at any time and turn it into your priority.

- Our body is like a house whose structures and systems can collapse if neglected.

- There is a great connection between your brain, your intestinal tract and your emotions.

- The gut microbiome, which is the bacteria found in the gastrointestinal tract, has been found to play an indispensable role in our health.

- Food and other supplements going through the gut indirectly feed the mind, which indirectly affects your entire mood and behavior.

- Your diet can be tweaked to help your thinking and mood and to give you the energy you need to become your desired best self.

- There is a need for you to reexamine your beliefs around diet and nutrition.

- The type of meals you eat determine whether you are fueling your anti self or your best self.

- Fermented food like kombucha is recommended as the type of food to incorporate into your daily diet in order to become your best self. Other recommendations are probiotic supplements, sauerkraut, kefir, unsweetened yoghurt and fiber. Also try to eat an apple daily.

- Interval fasting is also recommended as it induces autophagy. Autophagy is a situation where the body consumes its own tissue through a sort of recycling by using the waste produced by the body to create new materials needed for regeneration of the cells.

- Exercise is of numerous critical benefits to the human body, brain and spirit. Exercise is a key element in becoming your best self.

SUMMARY

The story is told of James who loves consuming calories until he became too fat for his health. The problem started at childhood. He was able to cover up his weakness through jokes and became loved by all. He tried losing the weight at a point in order to get a girlfriend. When she left him he relapsed again into his addiction of over eating. At thirty five, he took a drastic step and changed his diet in order to get good health.

While some of our health challenges reflect who we really are, others are a direct reflection of our habits. There are certain behaviors that affect our health: this can be alcohol, stress, lack of sleep, smoking etc. There are also some eating habits or foods that affect our health such taking too little water, sugary drinks, fried foods, lack of balanced diet and so on. There are fitness issues that can affect our health. For instance, not engaging in regular workout or engaging in a workout that can impair our health.

Gut feelings

There is some sort of relationship between your brain, intestinal tract and emotions. This is why you feel your stomach twisting when you are anxious or afraid. Your gut includes your digestive system. There are several billions of bacteria living in our gut and they have the tendency to control our mind. They play an important role in our health by keeping it balanced. If these gut bacteria are in the right proportion, they keep us in good health but if otherwise, they affect our immune system.

Whatever you put into your body has a way of affecting your output. All processed foods have negative effects on your health and cannot help you become your best self.

There are some foods we can consume to help us live healthy and become what we are destined to be. Some of these are: fermented foods like kombucha, unsweetened yoghurt and kefir. Probiotics supplements and sauerkraut are also good. And don't forget to consume an apple daily.

CHAPTER 8: YOUR EDUCATION/ LEARNING

KEY TAKEAWAYS

- I was not such a good student. I could not cope academically. For me school was torture. Things, however, changed for me when I went into mental health. I became very interested in this area of study. It clearly connected to my best self. I became more focused, started studying hard and became a straight "A" student. What changed was my ability to connect to my best self through mental health courses.

- Any time a person changes his or her story and goes after what he or she loves, amazing things happen. My sudden change in academics may appear as a miracle but in real sense, living right makes miracles real.

- You won't abuse drugs if you are or become happy with your life in general.

- Immediately you discover your passionate topics, learning will become easier.

- Education helps us to grow, to get better and to evolve.

- Endeavor to discover the areas of study, topics and things that interest you because those are what your best self is interested in.
- When you build new skills or learn new information, you are utilizing your brain in a new way. And through the science of neuroplasticity, you are changing the function and even the structure of your brain. Learning new skills, information, things etc helps your brain in the long run. It slows aging, keeps your brain clear and functioning at optimal levels. It also reduces the risk of getting dementia.
- Ensure you're always in the mood for learning because each new day brings a new opportunity for you to make improvements in your life and on those around you.

SUMMARY

I had been performing poorly academically from childhood. I only did well in basketball and socializing. I did so badly academically but I knew how to get over. I knew when report cards would be mailed out to students' homes. So I would always try to run ahead of the mail and intercept the report before anyone else in my home gets them.

It always worked for me, but I was not so lucky in my eight grade. On that occasion, before I could get home, the envelope containing my school results was already on the table. And while my siblings were rejoicing at their straight A's, I performed below expectation as usual resulting in my parents suggesting that I repeat the eighth grade, but in another school.

This failing streak and underperformance continued until I got to college, and then I started doing drugs. This led to my dropping out of school. However I sobered up and enrolled in another university. It was in my psychology and mental health courses that I connected with my best self and then, I started making straight A's.

I'm sharing this story of my fortunes with schooling and education to let you know that once you discover a topic or area of study which you are passionate about, you will love to learn. For me that area of study is mental health. I have since gone into the mental health profession, and ever since I have been so passionate to learn everything about mental health. My passion for this area of study is unremitting. It just connects with my best self.

There are people who may not like school but when they discover what interests them, they learn because our best self is always thirsty to know more.

Write down things and skills you will love to learn and state your reason(s) for not learning them such as age factor, lack of time or poor learning skill.

Learning should be done through love and not duty

Don't waste your time learning a skill or studying what you are not passionate about. Sometimes the universe has a way of intervening and stopping us when we are going astray. At other times, we should quit going in a particular direction if it's all struggling, without any sense of fulfillment.

CHAPTER 9: YOUR RELATIONSHIPS

KEY TAKEAWAYS

- Being at our best self at every point of interaction in any relationship can make the relationship easier to manage.
- The ability to align your values with your best self is of great benefit in making general life decisions as well as in relationships.
- Embrace positive values that depict the strength of your character than the negative ones that represent your anti self.
- The emotions of bitterness and unforgiveness towards your family members can spill over to other relationships.
- It is not possible to be different persons in different relationships. To be your best self, you must show up as such in all relationships.
- It is imperative to be aware of who you are and what you desire so you can grow in your relationship.
- The society and social media give us skewed expectations regarding what love and romance are

from childhood, and at adulthood. We feel disappointed when we meet with the reality of romance and love are in real life.

- There are intimate-relationship myths that your best self truth can help you to debunk.
- You can be single and still be your best self without any intimate relationship.
- There is no perfect relationship because we are all imperfect.
- There are parenting tools that parents can adopt in order to be their best self. Such tools include: good communication, rewarding kids appropriately, and parenting by negotiation, parenting by example and so on.

SUMMARY

This chapter focuses on your values, family relationships and intimate relationships. It discusses how you can get connected with your best self in all your relationships with people (whether they are in their best self or not).

Your Values

Our core values may be those principles and standards of living handed down to us by our parents. We might have adopted some but are they positive or negative? Embrace the positive ones and discard the negative ones. As you grow and see the changes in life as well as other evolvement, your values may change too. This is why your values need to be redefined from time to time to suit and align with those changes. Another challenge here is when your values are tested through a wrong accusation or through an unpleasant event.

Family relationships

The bonds we created with our family while growing have a way of shaping our behaviors and beliefs. It also affects our pattern of life all through life. A secure attachment is one where a parent or guardian gives a child the needed love and attention while an insecure one happens in opposite directions. However, a child can still grow up to become responsible even in the midst of insecure attachment. There are complex issues in family relationships that require the help of professionals to get the right healing. This includes abuse, which may negatively impact our lives.

Intimate relationships

This is the type of relationship between you and your spouse, partner, someone you are dating and others in that circle. It can be somehow difficult to align two different values coming from intimate relationships. This is why communication and openness play significant roles. Ensure that those within your intimate relationships share and respect your core values.

There is no parent that can do the job well without being in their best self. Parenting tools include; good communication, parenting by change, parenting by negotiation, parenting by example among others. Yelling at kids should be avoided while gratitude should be encouraged.

CHAPTER 10: YOUR EMPLOYMENT

KEY TAKEAWAYS

- There are two types of employees; those working for money and the passionate ones. The best and happiest employees are those who are passionate about what they do, who have aligned their jobs with their best self.

- When operating in my *why* I don't feel frustrated neither do I see my work as burdensome or time consuming. Since everyone is an artist, the *why* explains the art aspect.

- If your chosen career reflects your art, you will feel less exhaustion and more energy.

- Your lifestyle should determine the type of job you do. For instance, I'm not a paper working type but a people oriented person. That's why I love what I do because it dictates the right way for my real self.

- For employment applicants, learn everything possible about the company you're applying to or that is calling you for interview. Your knowledge of the company at this stage could be an indication of your level of passion.

- As an employee, put yourself in the shoes of the boss of the company and always come up with fresh ideas that can help move the company forward. By doing so, the boss will eventually reward your efforts and contributions.

SUMMARY

The question is often asked of kids about what they would like to become when they grow up. What a difference it would make if schools offered personal development courses for students and guided students to focus more on their natural gifts and how to discover themselves, instead of forcing courses down students' throats.

Work is not solely for money neither should you be afraid of it. Your goal in life is to make your work align with your real self. In order to discover what works for you, you must know what does not work for you.

CHAPTER 11: YOUR SPIRITUAL LIFE

KEY TAKEAWAYS

- Your spirituality is different from religion. I practice my religion through meditation, mantras, self affirmations and other routines.

- By getting connected and reconnecting to our past or lost spiritual selves and leaning on our faith, we get amazed at how fast things happen around us.

- As humans, we have our ways of putting ourselves into unseen boxes, which block us from seeing other bigger and higher opportunities around us.

SUMMARY

Your spiritual life serves as the foundation on which you build other SPHERES. I believe your best self is in reality your spiritual self; where you form values, integrity and where all goodness/light emanates from.

Techniques for connecting/reconnecting with our spirituality

- Creating an intention around it
- Fanning the flames in your spirit
- Finding a noiseless place/moment
- Checking for signs
- Giving credit
- Sharing with others
- Having fun always
- Giving and paying it forward

There is no way you can have a best self without a vibrant dynamic spiritual life.

CHAPTER 12: ASSEMBLING YOUR BEST TEAM

KEY TAKEAWAYS

- Your team is your inner circle of people that cut across the earlier discussed SPHERES.
- Having a team is so important because we need other people in our lives and we cannot amount to anything in life alone.
- While your team does not exist only to help you, you must reciprocate in action too because you are a team member to someone else.
- The more open we are in meeting those who support us at being our best self, the more privileges and opportunities we get at meeting them.
- My time and energy are way too precious to spend on anyone who won't give back but I gently shift him or her out of his/her role on my team.
- Reduce your contact to the barest minimum with any family member not helping you be your best self because you don't have to hold on to a relationship that will harm you under the guise of obligation.
- Understanding your team's limitations and capabilities will help in knowing who to make use of at a particular time.

SUMMARY

Those around us have a great influence on us and our SPHERES. The depth, complexities and richness of our existence on this planet is defined by our relationship and connection with others. Your team refers to your inner circle and not all those you relate with can be there. The idea is creating a team around you for desired inspiration and encouragement in order to be your real self.

Group of people in your SPHERES

- Social. Friends and confidants
- Personal. People who help you look/feel good within such as therapists, hairdressers, counsellors, mentors etc.
- Health. Doctors and nurses
- Education. Teachers, lecturers, professors and other public figures
- Relations. Spouse, siblings, kids, in laws and other family members.
- Employment. Boss, colleagues, clients etc.
- Spiritual. Spiritual leaders and those within your spiritual circle.

No one is an island. It is through the interconnections between us that determine the magic. To deepen your experience in life and thrive in all SPHERES of life, you need the help of your team.

CHAPTER 13: SEVEN STEPS TO ACQUIRING YOUR BEST SELF GOALS

KEY TAKEAWAYS

- Ensure that each goal syncs with your best self and not your ego.
- Avoid procrastinating about your goals. Convert your *someday* to now.
- To change your life, start by changing how you spend your time.
- Write down areas you think you can create time in your schedule to include something that is currently displaced.
- Prioritize what you feel is important now to avoid regret in future.

SUMMARY

Assess all discussed SPHERES and check areas you need to work on. If it is under relationship or health etc, write down what you need to do to be your best self under each SPHERES. The next thing is to work on your team under each SPHERES and create appropriate goals on how to improve your teams within the SPHERES.

- Define your goals according to specific behaviors and events. Instead of saying my goal is to become happy, you can tie the happiness to your behavior or event like ***my goal is to travel overseas.***
- Express your goals in measurable terms. They should be quantifiable. For instance, I want to clean the house is vague. Rather, ***my goal is to clean the master bedroom and kitchen today.***
- Choose a goal within your control and not on someone else.
- Get a plan and strategize a program that will help you land your goal
- Define your goals in steps
- Assign a timeline/deadline to your goals
- Create accountability for progress toward each goal. Get your team or partner to monitor the progress of your goal and be accountable to him or her.
- Set goals around the SPHERES

CONCLUSION

KEY TAKEAWAYS

- The universe desires us to be original, to be our best self.

- Life surprises those connected to their best self.

- What matters most is this moment. Legacy can wait. In fact legacy is irrelevant. And the future is unpredictable. So act in the **NOW**.

- If you choose to grow, life will definitely open up to you beyond your imagination.

SUMMARY

Life is not a destination but a journey which is not within your control except by holding to it tightly, which invariably implies suffering.

This book was born from a series of television shows with Dr. Phil and his audience on best self. He advised me to put the ideas into paper because he felt they were amazing and helpful. You can only get to the highest level and become best when you get in touch with the best side of you.

NOTES

NOTES

NOTES

NOTES

RECOMMENDED BY BOOKNATION

Summary of Atomic Habits by James Clear: An Easy & Proven Way to Build Good Habits & Break Bad Ones By BookNation Publishing

Summary Can't Hurt Me by David Goggins: Master Your Mind and Defy the Odds By Bob "Sarge" Kessone

CPSIA information can be obtained
at www.ICGtesting.com
Printed in the USA
BVHW031354060519
547457BV00012B/1747/P